BOY SCOUTS OF AMERICA
MERIT BADGE SERIES

WOODWORK

 BOY SCOUTS OF AMERICA.

Requirements

1. Do the following:

   a. Show that you know first aid for injuries that could occur while woodworking, including splinters, scratches, cuts, severe bleeding, and shock. Tell what precautions must be taken to help prevent loss of eyesight or hearing, and explain why and when it is necessary to use a dust mask.

   b. Earn the Totin' Chip recognition.

   c. Tell your counselor what precautions you take to safely use your tools.

2. Do the following:

   a. Describe how timber is grown, harvested, and milled. Tell how lumber is cured, seasoned, graded, and sized.

   b. Collect and label blocks of six kinds of wood useful in woodworking. Describe the chief qualities of each. Give the best uses of each.

3. Do the following:

   a. Show the proper care, use, and storage of all working tools and equipment that you own or use at home or school.

   b. Sharpen correctly the cutting edges of two different tools.

4. Using a saw, plane, hammer, brace, and bit, make something useful of wood. Cut parts from lumber that you have squared and measured from working drawings.

35968
ISBN 978-0-8395-3316-0
©2003 Boy Scouts of America
2010 Printing

BANG/Brainerd, MN
4-2010/059767

5. Create your own carpentry project. List the materials you will need to complete your project, and then build your project. Keep track of the time you spend and the cost of the materials.

6. Do any TWO of the following:

   a. Make working drawings of a project needing (1) beveled or rounded edges OR curved or incised cuttings, OR (2) miter, dowel, or mortise and tenon joints. Build this project.

   b. Make something for which you have to turn duplicate parts on a lathe.

   c. Make a cabinet, box, or something else with a door or lid fastened with inset hinges.

   d. Help make and repair wooden toys for underprivileged children OR help carry out a carpentry service project approved by your counselor for a charitable organization.

7. Talk with a cabinetmaker or carpenter. Find out about the training, apprenticeship, career opportunities, work conditions, work hours, pay rates, and union organization that woodworking experts have in your area.

Contents

Trees and Wood

All the wood around you and all the wood you will use in your woodworking projects was once part of a living tree. Trees use water and minerals from the soil, carbon dioxide from the air, and energy from sunlight to make wood.

Wood is an amazingly versatile, practical, yet beautiful material. It can become a roof over our heads, a floor beneath our feet, a fun toy or piece of art, a musical instrument—just about anything. As a woodworker or carpenter, you will find no end of useful, valuable, and fun items you can make yourself, from wood.

The *grain* of wood is its pattern of lines, curves, and shadings. The grain pattern is caused by the tree's growth. Usually the grain runs lengthwise in boards. The grain showing at either end of a board is called *end grain*. The wide surface of a board is its *face,* the narrow surface its *edge.*

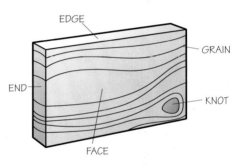

Kinds of Wood

A good way to start on the Woodwork merit badge is to collect and label blocks of six kinds of wood useful in woodworking. You may be able to get small samples from a carpenter, cabinetmaker, lumberyard, building center, or home project center. Scavenge for scrap wood from the garage or workshop of a family member or friend. (No matter how small the scrap, ask before taking it.) If you are able to identify the branches of deadwood you find while hiking, you can use those, too.

Wood is divided into two main groups. **Hardwoods** come from broadleaf trees, which usually lose their leaves in autumn. Hardwoods include oak, ash, hickory, maple, tulip tree, sweet gum, birch, tupelo, aspen, walnut, cherry, and beech. **Softwoods** come from trees called *conifers,* which have waxy needles or scalelike leaves that they keep through the winter. For this reason, they are also called evergreens. Pines, Douglas fir, Western true firs, hemlock, redwood, spruce, and cedars are softwoods.

The point of requirement 2b is to get familiar with these different kinds of woods, their major qualities, and their main uses. Use this chart to guide you in collecting samples, and try for variety in your collection.

Hardwoods

Wood	Chief Qualities	Major Uses
American Elm	Tough, hard, does not split easily; usually light brown in color	Hockey sticks, butcher blocks, barrels, fence posts, furniture, boats
American Tulipwood (Yellow Poplar)	Lightweight, straight-grained, moderately stiff, very stable when dried, easy to work	Interior trim, furniture, picture frames, toys
Basswood (American Linden)	Lightweight, soft, even-textured, durable	Boxes, baskets, furniture, toys, woodcarvings
Beech	Hard, close-grained, tough	Furniture, wooden tools, tool handles, veneers
Birch	Fairly strong, hard, fine-grained, easy to work	Furniture, dowels, interior trim, kitchen cabinets
Black Walnut	Strong, hard, heavy, dark, fine-grained	Fine furniture, cabinets, interior trim, veneers, gunstocks
Cherry	Strong, hard, stable, fine-grained	Fine furniture and cabinets
Hickory	Strong, hard, close-grained, flexible	Tool handles, baseball bats, furniture
Mahogany	Strong, durable, moderately hard, heavy; easy to work, stable, does not readily shrink, swell, or warp; prized for its rich, reddish-brown color and beautiful grain	Fine furniture, trim, veneers
Oak	Heavy, very strong, hard; one of the most durable woods	Heavy furniture, cabinets, railroad ties, floors, beams, other building parts
Sugar Maple	Strong, heavy, hard, light-colored, close-grained, durable	Floors, bowling alleys, furniture, musical instruments, interior trim, cutting boards
White Ash	Strong, hard, elastic; a great shock absorber	Baseball bats, tool handles, oars, furniture

Softwoods

Wood	Chief Qualities	Major Uses
Douglas Fir	Strong, stable wood for construction	House-building, structural lumber, railroad ties
Eastern Hemlock	Soft, light, splintery	Clapboards, framing lumber
Red Cedar	Soft, easy to work; a fragrant, durable wood, very stable, resists rotting and repels insects	Closet linings, cigar boxes, shingles, cedar chests, telephone poles, posts, siding
Redwood	Brownish red, soft but durable, resists decay and insects; easy to work	Exterior trim, siding, outdoor furniture, decks
Spruce	Strong, light, flexible	Canoe paddles, musical instruments, ship masts and spars, boxes, interior trim, framing lumber
White Pine	Soft, smooth-grained, easy to work	Interior trim, doors
Yellow Pine	Durable, strong, straight-grained; harder and more difficult to work than white pine	Structural lumber, knotty paneling

Plywood and Veneers

One of the most useful materials in woodworking is *plywood*, a sandwich of three or more thin sheets of wood. The sheets, called *veneers*, are glued and pressed together, with the grain directions alternating, to form one solid sheet. This arrangement makes plywood strong.

You can buy plywood that has a *face veneer*, or thin outside sheet, of fine wood such as mahogany or walnut. This gives an expensive look that is less costly. Plywood and veneers are widely used in construction and in cabinetmaking.

If you use a piece of plywood as one of your samples for requirement 2b, be sure you know what wood is used for the face veneer.

A **cabinetmaker** is a skilled woodworker who makes fine furniture.

Timber and Lumber

Standing trees and their wood are called *timber*. Timber cut and prepared for use is *lumber*. In the United States, timber is harvested from public (national and state) forests and from private forests owned by companies that manufacture lumber, paper, and other wood products. Foresters grow and harvest crops of trees much as farmers raise corn, wheat, or other crops.

Field crops ripen in a year or less. Trees, however, may grow for five to 30 years or longer before they are ready for cutting. The business of growing and harvesting timber takes patience.

For more about forest management, see the *Forestry* merit badge pamphlet.

Planting Trees

Timber may grow from seeds or from seedlings. To scatter seeds on forest land, airplanes or helicopters generally are used. But people working with hand tools may also plant tree seeds in the ground.

Seedlings (young trees) are raised in a nursery for one to four years before being transplanted to the forest. Foresters use hand tools or planting machines to plant seedlings.

Harvesting Timber

The four main methods of harvesting timber are selection cutting, shelterwood cutting, clearcutting, and seed tree cutting.

Selection Cutting. Harvesters take small patches of mature trees, usually trees that are large and growing near others. Foresters leave many larger trees in place, however, to make seeds. Removing mature trees creates room for younger trees to grow. Forests may be harvested by selection cutting every five to 30 years. American beech, sugar maple, and hemlock are some of the trees typically harvested by this method.

Selection cutting

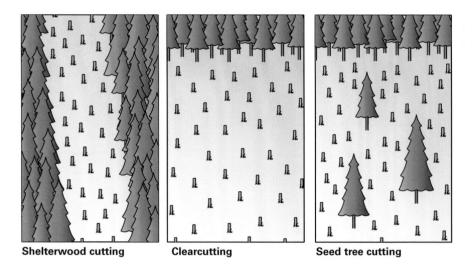

Shelterwood cutting   Clearcutting   Seed tree cutting

Shelterwood Cutting. A stand (area) of timber is harvested in stages over a span of 10 to 20 years. Foresters plant new trees where the mature ones are cut down. This method is called "shelterwood" because the trees left standing provide shelter (shade) for the newly planted trees. Some trees, such as oak, ponderosa pine, and white pine, need shade during their early growing years.

Clearcutting. Clearcutting is removing all the trees from a section of forest. Clearcut areas can be a few acres or hundreds of acres large. Foresters may replant the area, or new trees sprout from the stumps of the old ones. The seedlings that replace the harvested trees grow in full sunlight. They produce a stand of trees all the same age.

Seed Tree Cutting. This method resembles clearcutting, except a few trees are left scattered through the cutover area as a natural source of seeds. Loblolly pine, longleaf pine, and other southern pines can be grown using this method.

Milling Lumber

Loggers cut down trees that foresters have marked for cutting. Then workers called *buckers* lop off the limbs and slice the trunks into shorter lengths (logs) that are easier to handle.

The logs are trucked, floated, or carried on railroads to a *sawmill*. At the mill, logs are debarked (their bark is removed), and saws cut them into boards (lumber).

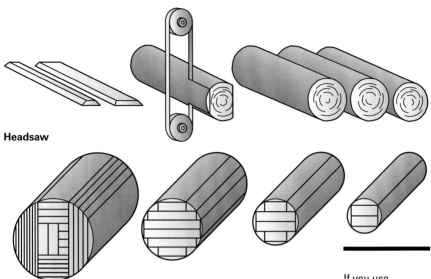

Headsaw

Large and small logs are sawed in various patterns to get as much lumber as possible from each log.

Small logs are often cut into boards in a single pass through a set of saws (a *gangsaw*) that makes many cuts at once. Large logs may make several passes through one saw (a *headsaw*) that slices off a board at a time until the whole log is cut into lumber. The new lumber, called *green lumber*, is edged and trimmed to straighten the sides and cut into boards of standard lengths.

Grading Lumber

Lumber is graded for quality, appearance, and strength. In the case of hardwoods, the amount of usable wood or "clear" wood (wood without defects such as knots, holes, or splits) determines the grade of a piece of lumber.

HARDWOOD GRADES

The seven grades of hardwood lumber, from highest to lowest, are Firsts and Seconds (FAS), Selects, No. 1 Common, No. 2 Common, No. 3A Common, No. 3B Common, and Sound Wormy.

If you use hardwood in your woodworking projects, it probably will be graded FAS, Selects, or No. 1 Common. Woodworkers seldom see the lower grades. Manufacturers use them to make flooring, pallets, and similar products.

The term *yard lumber* is often used for the nonstress-graded and appearance lumber sold in lumberyards. This is the type of softwood lumber many woodworkers use.

SOFTWOOD GRADES

For softwoods, there are almost as many grading systems as there are kinds of wood. All systems, however, follow the basic rule that *the fewer the blemishes and the nicer the color and grain, the better and more expensive the wood.* The top grades ("A" or "No. 1") have practically no defects. The middle grades may have a few knots and some variations in color. The lowest grades (usually "D," "No. 4," or "No. 5") may have large knots and even knotholes.

Here are some of the softwood grades you may find at a lumberyard or building center.

Appearance graded lumber is for interior trim, paneling, flooring, cabinetwork, and the like. The grades are shown by letters: A, B, C, D, and combination grades such as "B and better" ("B&B" or "B&BTR") and "C and better" ("C&BTR"). Depending on the kind of wood, appearance grades may also be called "Select," "Finish," "Superior," "Prime," or "Clear."

Nonstress-graded (common) lumber is used where strength is not crucial for safety. Boards in this group are often used for siding, shelving, and paneling. The grades for this "common lumber" may be numbered or named, as No. 1 (Construction), No. 2 (Standard), No. 3 (Utility), or No. 4 and No. 5 (Economy).

Stress-graded (dimension) lumber is *structural lumber* graded according to the load it can carry. Structural lumber (referred to as "dimension" lumber) must be strong for use as posts, beams, studs, and rafters. The grades for dimension lumber (2" x 4" and wider) range from Select Structural (abbreviated SEL STR) through Nos. 1–3 and Construction, Standard, and Utility.

PLYWOOD GRADES

Plywood comes in three grades. **Rough** plywood is rough to the touch, knotty, and the least expensive. **Finish** plywood is smoother, with a finer surface. It costs more than rough plywood. **Exterior-grade** plywood is made especially for use outdoors. Waterproof glue keeps its layers from separating or buckling if the wood gets wet.

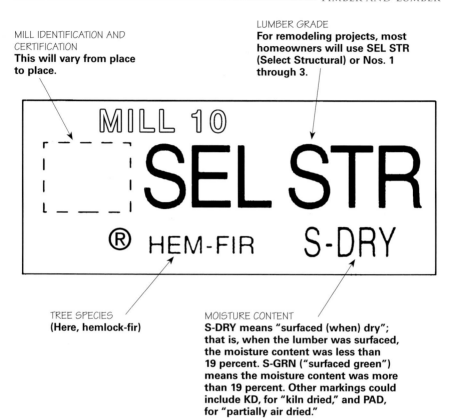

MILL IDENTIFICATION AND CERTIFICATION
This will vary from place to place.

LUMBER GRADE
For remodeling projects, most homeowners will use SEL STR (Select Structural) or Nos. 1 through 3.

TREE SPECIES
(Here, hemlock-fir)

MOISTURE CONTENT
S-DRY means "surfaced (when) dry"; that is, when the lumber was surfaced, the moisture content was less than 19 percent. S-GRN ("surfaced green") means the moisture content was more than 19 percent. Other markings could include KD, for "kiln dried," and PAD, for "partially air dried."

©Penn State College of Agricultural Sciences, Agriculture Information Services, courtesy; illustration by Thomas Laird, AV & Exhibit Graphics Specialist

Seasoning Lumber

To *season* (or *cure*) lumber is to dry it. Wood will warp if too much moisture is left in it. Some lumber is seasoned by *air drying.* It's stacked outdoors to dry by sun and wind. *Kiln drying* is quicker. Green lumber goes into drying sheds, or *kilns,* where the temperature and the moisture in the air are controlled. Blowers in the shed circulate warm air, drying the lumber with more consistency in a few days than would be possible during months of air drying.

Sizing Lumber

Lumber comes in standard sizes, with the thickness and width measured in inches and the length in feet. Lumber is measured before it is seasoned and *surfaced* (made smooth). Lumber shrinks as it dries, and smoothing the surface also makes the finished pieces smaller than their *nominal* (named) size.

Therefore, if you go to a building center or lumberyard and ask for an 8-foot "two-by-four," should you expect to get a piece of lumber that is 8 feet long, 2 inches thick, and 4 inches wide? No. The two-by-four will be a full 8 feet long. Even though the actual thickness and width of the board may be only $1^1/2$" x $3^1/2$", it still is called a "two-by-four."

Standard Sizes of Wood

Nominal Size	Actual Thickness	Actual Width
1" x 4"	$3/4$"	$3^1/2$"
2" x 4"	$1^1/2$"	$3^1/2$"
1" x 6"	$3/4$"	$5^1/2$"
1" x 12"	$3/4$"	$11^1/4$" or $11^1/2$"

These are some common lumber sizes you may use in your projects. Wood comes in other standard sizes. Take a tape measure on your next trip to the lumberyard or building center and check the actual dimensions and nominal sizes of the lumber sold there.

Standard lumber sizes vary depending on moisture content and the type of wood. Hardwood is sold in lengths that can be divided evenly into 1-foot sections. Softwood structural lumber is sold in lengths divisible into 2-foot sections. Dimension lumber is typically 2 inches thick and up to 12 inches wide. (The two-by-four in the above example is dimension lumber.) Board lumber is typically 1 inch thick and up to 12 inches wide. Timbers (defined in this sense as "large squared pieces of wood") measure 5 or more inches thick.

Woodworkers and carpenters sometimes use another measurement of wood, called a *board foot*. To find out how many board feet are in a piece of lumber, multiply the length of the lumber (in feet) by the thickness (in inches) by the width (in feet). If you know the width in inches, divide by 12 to convert to feet.

For example, to figure the board feet in a 10-foot 1" x 6":

10' x 1" x $6/12$ = 5 board feet

Now you try it. How many board feet are in an 8-foot 2" x 4"?

8' x 2" x $4/12$ = ? (Find the answer at the end of this chapter.)

Composite Woods

Composite woods are made from wood and at least one other material. Most are made by combining wood or bits of wood with an adhesive resin or glue.

In your woodworking projects, you may use some of these composite woods:

- **Plywood**—made from plies (veneers or layers) of wood glued together

- **Particleboard**—made from wood flakes, shavings, and similar particles of wood glued together with synthetic resin and pressed into stable sheets

- **Medium density fiberboard (MDF)**—made from fine, individual wood fibers or fiber bundles bonded with adhesive to give a smooth, flat face and clean, easily workable edges

- **Oriented strandboard (OSB)**—made from thin strands of wood that are glued and pressed into a solid panel

- **Hardboard**—made from wood pulp and particles that are squeezed, glued, and dried into panels with a density higher than particleboard or MDF

The panel products usually are sold in 4' x 8' sheets, $1/8$ inch and up in thickness. Some plywoods are $3/4$ inch and even thicker. Plywood up to $3/8$ inch usually has three plies or layers. Thicker plywoods have five or sometimes seven layers.

How many board feet are in an 8-foot 2" x 4"?
8' x 2" x $4/12$ = 5.33 board feet

Tools and How to Use Them

Learn the skillful and safe use of your woodworking tools. Learn to use the right tool for the job—it makes working with wood easier, safer, and faster. And learn to take care of tools to keep them working longer. This chapter gives you a rundown on useful tools and how to select, use, and care for them correctly and safely.

Some of your woodwork projects may go more quickly if you can use power tools (see below). But if you prefer to work only with hand tools (as many fine woodworkers do), you can successfully complete all requirements for the badge. The choice is yours. It may depend, of course, on what tools are available to you.

Measuring and Leveling Tools

Tape measure

A **rule** is essential for measuring wood. A *folding rule* is a collapsible, usually 6-foot, rigid wooden ruler. A steel *tape measure* has a flexible metal blade, 16 feet to 33 feet or longer, that rolls up in a case. For small jobs, you may use a yardstick or a common 12-inch ruler.

How to Use a Rule

Lay a rule on edge so that the marks showing divisions of inches are flush against the wood. Use a plain soft-lead pencil to mark measurements. The wide lead of carpenter's pencils makes too broad a mark. Mark a measurement not with a dot but with a dash going in the direction of the cutting line you plan to draw.

Squares are for marking or checking right angles. A *try square* is shaped like an L with a perfect 90-degree (right) angle. Often made with a metal blade and a wooden handle, a try square is used to check that corners are square and edges are straight.

Try square

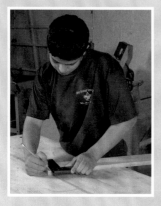

How to Use a Try Square

Hold a try square's thick handle against one edge of a board so that the thin blade hooks over the board's end. If the end of the board doesn't align precisely with the edge of the blade, the board isn't square.

To square the board, hold the try square's handle firmly against one edge of the board so that the metal blade lies flat across the board's face, about 2 inches from the crooked end. Pencil a line along the blade from edge to edge of the board. Lay the board on your workbench or other work surface, making sure that the pencil line clears the edge of the bench by about 2 inches. Clamp the board to the bench. Saw along the pencil line to remove the board's crooked end.

Carpenter's square   **Combination square**   **Level**

The larger, all-metal *carpenter's square,* also called a *framing square,* can be used to mark boards that are too broad for the try square.

The *combination square* has a movable handle that locks in place on its 12-inch steel rule. It can be used like a try square to square the end of a board. Or it can be used to mark a 45-degree angle (half of 90 degrees).

A *level* is used for checking whether a board, shelf, or other work piece is exactly level (horizontal) or plumb (vertical; straight up and down). Another tool for checking verticality is the **plumb line,** which is a string with a weight on its end. When a plumb line hangs freely, it makes an exactly vertical line.

Fastening Tools

Hammers come in
many styles and sizes.
A basic *claw hammer*
has a forked, curved
end opposite the head.
A 10-ounce claw ham-
mer or one not much
heavier may be your
best choice.

Claw hammer

How to Use a Hammer

To start a nail, hold the nail by the shank (the
straight part), well below the head. Lightly tap
the head two or three times so the nail is driven
just far enough into the wood to stand by itself. Then
move your hand clear.

To drive the nail deeper, swing your arm at the elbow, hit the
nail head squarely, and hammer only until the head is flush with the
surface of the wood. Any farther and the head of the hammer may
damage the wood surface.

To remove a bent nail, use the forked end of a claw hammer.
Hold the hammer upside down and slide the notch of the fork under

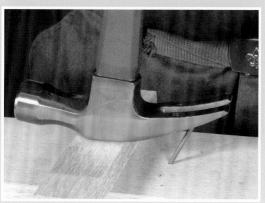

the head of the
nail. Use a block of
scrap wood under
the hammer's head
if you need to raise
the hammer high
enough for the
claws to catch the
nail head. Then pull
back on the handle
to pull the nail from
the wood.

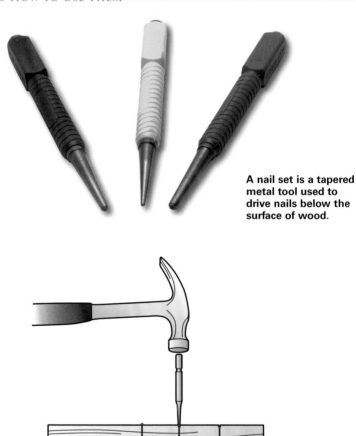

A nail set is a tapered metal tool used to drive nails below the surface of wood.

How to Use a Nail Set

A nail set is used most often with thin, small-headed nails, called *finishing nails,* for projects that will be stained and varnished rather than painted. Drive a finishing nail as close to the wood surface as you can without denting the wood with the hammer. Then place the nail set on the nail head and tap the head below the surface. Fill the hole with wood filler to hide the nail.

A **mallet** is a hammer with a head usually made of wood or rubber and is used for hitting wood but never for driving nails. If you have to tap dowels in using a claw hammer, be careful not to split the wood.

Common nails, for general construction work, have large, round, flat heads. *Box nails* have a narrower shank and are used to avoid splitting thin wood. See "Nail Types" and "Nail Sizes" in the *Home Repairs* merit badge pamphlet.

Mallet

Screwdrivers come in two main different types. A *standard screwdriver* has a flat tip or blade for driving single-slotted screws. A *Phillips screwdriver* has a cross-shaped tip for driving cross-slotted screws.

Screws also have different shapes of heads: flat, round, or oval. You will probably use flathead wood screws most. They can be seated so the head is flush (level) with the wood surface. Or they can be *countersunk* (driven below the surface) and filled over to hide the head.

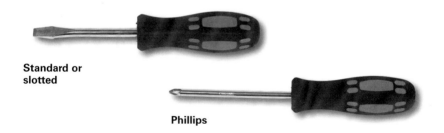

Standard or slotted

Phillips

How to Use a Screwdriver

Match the screwdriver to the screw. Use the right tip, and also the correct size. A blade too thick won't fit in the screw slot. A blade too wide may scratch the wood surface. A blade too narrow can twist in the screw slot, slip out, and gouge the wood or stab you.

Wood hand-screw clamps are useful for holding pieces of wood together while you join them with nails, screws, or glue. Clamps also secure wood to a workbench or table. In place of clamps, use a **vise** attached to a workbench.

How to Use a Clamp

Always secure wood, using clamps or a vise as needed, before cutting or otherwise working with it. If you use a machinist's vise, use scrap wood to protect your good wood from the vise's teeth.

Cutting Tools

A **ripsaw** is for cutting a piece of wood lengthwise, in the direction of the grain. A **crosscut saw** is for cutting across the grain, as when you saw the end off a board. A **backsaw,** which has a thin blade stiffened by a metal bar along its back, is for precise cutting and fine work.

How to Use a Crosscut Saw

Point your index finger along the side of the saw handle for better control and to cut a straighter, truer line. To start the cut, set the saw blade on the far edge of the wood (that is, the corner where the face and the edge meet).

How to hold a crosscut saw.

Pull the saw back toward you a few times, making a groove. Then saw back and forth, cutting with long, smooth strokes, angling the saw toward the ground. An even rhythm is more important than speed. Keep your forearm and the saw blade in line. Follow your cutting line and keep the blade square to the board, not leaning left or right.

Japanese Saws

A conventional handsaw, which cuts on the push stroke, has a fairly thick blade to withstand the pushing force. *Japanese saws,* in contrast, cut on the pull stroke. Because there is

Japanese saw

less strain on them, the blades won't buckle and can be thinner. A thin blade cuts faster, with less effort, and more control. If pull-stroke saws are available to you, try them. Like many other woodworkers, you may find them easier to use than ordinary handsaws.

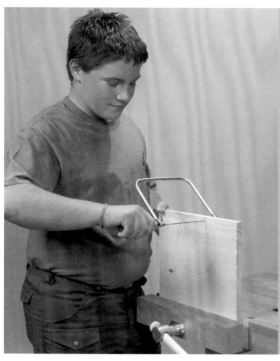

How to Use a Coping Saw

To make a cutout in a piece of wood, first bore a hole, 1/4" or larger, just inside the shape you want to cut out. Remove the blade of the coping saw, slip the blade through the bored hole, and replace the blade in the saw frame. With the blade thus "inside" the wood, saw along the cutting line.

A coping saw is good for cutting curves. Its thin, replaceable blade can be angled.

How to Use a Rasp

A rasp works only as it's moving forward. Push it across the surface to be smoothed, and then pick it up and bring it back.

A rasp has sharp teeth for smoothing rough surfaces.

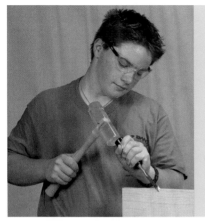

How to Use a Chisel

Do not cut too deeply. Chisels are meant to chip and shave away wood. Start the blade digging gently into the wood, slightly inside your guideline mark. If you need to use more pressure than you can apply by hand, tap the chisel's handle with a wooden mallet. Always aim the cutting edge away from your body and hands.

Use a chisel to pare out wood for a hinge.

Chisels have strong, square, flat blades with beveled (slanting) edges for shaving and shaping wood. The wedge of a chisel's blade cuts and lifts unwanted wood out of the way.

Planes are for smoothing and straightening rough or uneven surfaces, or for shaving extra thickness or width from a piece of wood. A *smoothing plane* is the most common. The longer *jack plane* is for planing long pieces of wood. A *block plane,* the shortest, is for smoothing the end grain or trimming small pieces of wood. A block plane is normally held and used with one hand.

A block plane can be used for beveling edges. See project 5 for a picture of a bevel.

Vary the downward pressure when you plane a board.

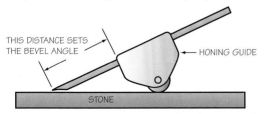

THIS DISTANCE SETS THE BEVEL ANGLE

HONING GUIDE

STONE

The main parts of a plane are the *sole* (base plate), the *handle,* the *knob,* and an adjustable *cutting iron* (blade).

How to Use a Plane

Secure the wood with a vise or clamps. Hold the plane with a hand on the handle and a hand on the knob. Push the plane firmly along the entire length of the wood without lifting it off the surface. Then raise the plane and move it back to the starting position. When starting cuts, apply more pressure to the front of the plane. When completing cuts, apply more pressure to the back.

Plane *with* (not against) the grain of the wood. If the plane sticks, digs in, or lifts chips of the wood, you are probably planing against the grain. Turn the wood around in the vise. Make sure only a little of the cutting blade sticks out of the base plate. Too much blade makes the plane hard to use and may damage the wood. Use a sharp blade. When you aren't using a plane, rest it on its side to avoid dulling the blade.

Drilling Tools

Drills hold bits (sharp metal points) to bore holes in wood. A **hand drill** holds cutting bits or twist drills for making holes up to $1/4$ inch in diameter. A **brace,** with its larger bits called auger bits, bores larger holes.

How to Use a Drill

Always drill with straight-in (not sideways) pressure to avoid bending or breaking the bit. To eliminate splintering when using a brace and bit, drill through one side of the wood until the tip of the bit shows, and then turn the wood over and bore from the other side to finish the hole.

In modern workshops, electric drills have largely replaced the traditional brace and bit. For requirement 4, however, you are to use a brace and bit even if you have an electric drill available. Using a brace and bit helps you understand the qualities of the wood you are working.

How to Use an Electric Drill

To start a hole, push the point of a nail into the wood to make a small dent. The dent will help keep the drill bit from skittering across the wood as you begin drilling. Put a thick piece of scrap wood under the drilling area to prevent damage to your workbench or table, in case the bit breaks through the underside of the wood you are drilling.

Let the drill do the drilling. Don't apply excessive pressure. Keep the drill running as you finish the hole and gently pull the bit out. Otherwise the bit may *bind* (stick in the hole) and you could bend or break the bit trying to get it free.

Use power tools only with constant and responsible adult supervision. Power tools are potentially dangerous tools.

Basic Power Tools

A popular size of **electric drill** is $3/8$ inch. It will accept bits in common sizes from $1/16$ inch up.

A **circular saw** has a round, disklike, toothed blade, with knobs to adjust the cutting angle and depth of the blade. The blade is normally set at a cutting depth of $1/8$ inch more than the thickness of the board you are sawing.

How to Use a Circular Saw

Keep the saw's baseplate flat on the surface of the wood to avoid binding. Be sure both ends of the board you are cutting are well supported, and don't cut between the supports. The end you are cutting (the scrap end) should stick out beyond one of the supports. This will keep the saw blade from binding when the cut board drops.

Circular saw

A **jigsaw** (also called a **saber saw**) has a single short, thin blade that moves rapidly up and down. With a saber saw you can cut curves, circles, inside edges, and decorative edges.

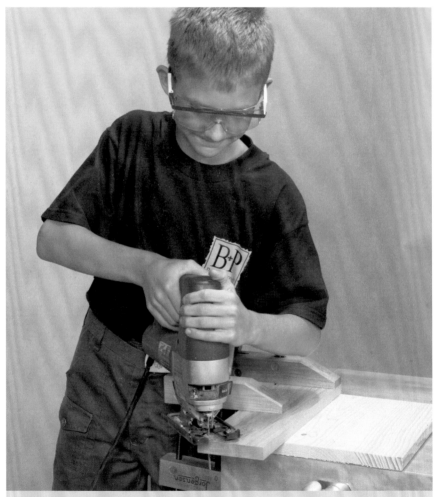

How to Use a Jigsaw

To start your cut from inside a piece of wood, first drill a starting hole, and then put the jigsaw blade through the hole.

A type of **power sander** popular with woodworkers is the *orbital sander,* sometimes called a *pad sander.* It has a flat sanding base that moves with short, quick strokes.

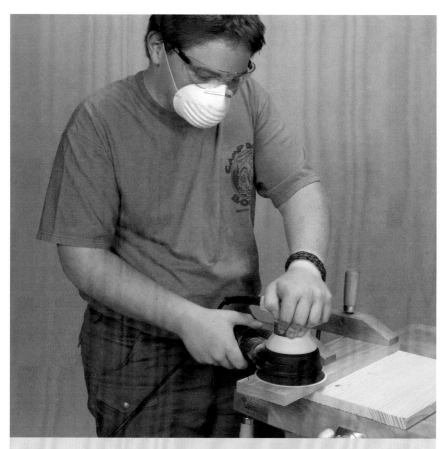

How to Use an Orbital Sander

Wear a dust mask. Do not press down on the sander. Let the tool's own weight do the sanding. To avoid gouging the wood, don't start or stop a power sander while it is on the wood. Keep the machine running as you set it down or lift it off. Keep the sander constantly moving over the wood's surface. Whenever possible, sand with the grain. Start with coarse sandpaper and finish with a fine paper.

More Tool Care Tips

- Keep your tools clean and properly lubricated. A film of rust-inhibiting oil will help protect tools from corrosion.

- Store metal tools safely indoors, never outside.

- Store tools out of the way when you aren't using them. Have a secure place for every tool and keep it in its place. Tools left lying around can get broken or pose a danger.

Safety Pointers

Tools designed for cutting, drilling, and shaping wood can slice through flesh in an instant. In addition, power tools can cause severe burns and electrical shock.

Keep yourself safe. Learn and take these precautions. (See additional safety tips in the *Home Repairs* merit badge pamphlet.)

Equipment and Clothing

- Always wear safety glasses when hammering, chiseling, or sanding or when using power tools.

- Wear hearing protectors when using power tools. Many power tools are noisy enough to damage your hearing.

- When sanding, sawing, or doing any work that produces wood dust, wear a disposable dust mask to avoid breathing sawdust.

- Don't wear loose clothing or jewelry that could catch in moving parts. Tie back long hair.

- Indoors, use glues, adhesives, paints, varnishes, etc., only with proper ventilation. Wear a face mask or respirator for protection against toxic fumes.

Materials and Procedures

- Secure wood—using clamps or a vise as needed—before drilling, cutting, or shaping it. When you saw a board, be sure both of its ends are well-supported (on a pair of sawhorses, for example). Don't cut between the supports.

- Keep your hands clear of blades, bits, and other cutting edges or moving parts.

- Never remove guards from machinery.

- Never use a power tool in wet or damp areas.

- Properly ground power tools. Plug them into three-hole grounded outlets.

General Safety

- Always work away from your body; that is, never point a sharp object, such as a screwdriver or chisel, toward you as you work.

- Always unplug power tools before changing their settings or parts. Keep a tool's adjustment key(s) taped to the power cord near the plug. This saves keys from getting lost and also reminds you to unplug the tool before you adjust it.

- Keep power cords away from blades, and otherwise make sure that the cord doesn't hinder the tool's operation.

- Keep a firm grip on hand-held power tools. They can get away from you if you are not in control.

- Watch what you are doing. Stop your work if something distracts you. Don't work with tools if you are tired or sleepy.

First Aid

Keep a first-aid kit on hand and know what to do for injuries that could occur while woodworking. The following is a quick review of the basics. For details, see the *First Aid* merit badge pamphlet and *The Boy Scout Handbook*.

Remove **splinters** with tweezers. Encourage the wound to bleed to flush out foreign matter. Wash with soap and water. Apply antiseptic. Cover with an adhesive bandage.

Wash **scratches and minor cuts** with soap and water. Apply antiseptic. Cover with an adhesive bandage.

For an **object in the eye,** do not rub the eye. Make tears flow by blinking or flush the eye with water to wash away the object. To remove an object from the white part of the eye, use the corner of a clean cloth or handkerchief. Do not try to take out something that is stuck in the eye. Cover the injured eye with a dry, sterile gauze pad and seek medical attention.

For **severe bleeding,** apply direct pressure to the wound. Raise the injury above the level of the heart. Seek medical help.

For **burns,** place in cold or cool water to reduce pain. Let the burn dry, and then protect it with a sterile gauze pad. If blisters form, do not break them. Do not apply butter, creams, ointments, or sprays. In the case of third-degree (severe) burns, treat for shock and seek immediate medical attention.

In case of **electric shock,** pull the plug or shut off the power at the main switch or breaker box. Do not directly touch a live wire or anyone in contact with a live current. Use a dry cloth to pull a live wire from a victim. To drag someone clear, use a cloth to pull the victim far enough to break contact. Then, if the person is not breathing, give rescue breathing (see the *First Aid* merit badge pamphlet). Send for emergency medical assistance.

Sharpening Cutting Edges

Keep the blades sharp on all your cutting tools. Dull blades are hard to use. You are more likely to mar your work and injure yourself with a dull blade than a sharp one because dull blades require extra force and can slip.

> Never throw tools into a toolbox. Rough handling will nick and dull the cutting edges.

Most wood-cutting tools have two wedge shapes on their cutting edge: the main or *ground bevel,* and the *sharpening bevel.* When you are sharpening an edge, you should be working off the sharpening bevel only, not the larger ground bevel.

When sharpening a blade, start with a rough stone, followed by (in this order and as needed) a medium, fine, and smooth stone. Finish with a piece of leather, commonly called a leather *strop.* (For more about sharpening stones and leather strops, see the *Wood Carving* merit badge pamphlet.)

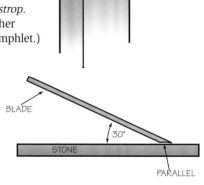

Sharpening a Plane

Take the plane apart and remove the cutting iron or blade. Lay the iron facedown on a whetstone. Then raise it slowly until you feel that it "fits"; that is, until you are sure both heel and toe (front and back) of the cutting edge are on the stone. *The sharpening angle must be parallel to the stone.* Whet the edge by pushing it forward over the stone.

To finish, turn the blade over on its flat side and, keeping the back flat on the stone, push it forward. Stoning both sides produces a little wiry burr on the edge. Remove the burr or wire edge by stropping on a piece of leather.

Correct angle for sharpening the cutting iron of a plane

Burr on a blade

Sharpening a Chisel

Use the same technique to sharpen a chisel, making sure you keep a constant angle as you push the chisel forward over the stone. You may tend to roll your hand, but it's vital to maintain the same angle. Pull the chisel back toward you with a light return stroke; apply no pressure. Stone both sides, and then remove the wire edge (burr) by stropping.

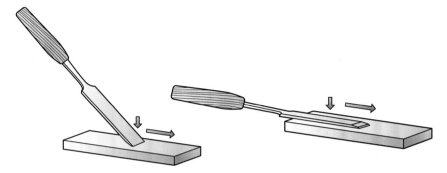

When you find the correct angle, remember it and keep it constant.

Turn the chisel over on its flat side and keep it absolutely flat as you stone the back.

This is to certify that the bearer

_____

has read the woods tools use and safety rules from the "Second Class Scout" chapter of the *Boy Scout Handbook.* He knows that the ownership or use of woods tools means responsibility, and he accepts it. In consideration of the above, he is hereby granted "Totin' Rights."

Scout leader _____

BOY SCOUTS ✠ OF AMERICA®

My Responsibility

I will take this card to my Scout leader or someone designated by my leader and do the following:

1. Read and understand woods tools use and safety rules from the *Boy Scout Handbook.*
2. Demonstrate proper handling, care, and use of the pocketknife, ax, and saw.
3. Use the knife, ax, and saw as tools, not playthings. Use them only when you are willing to give them your full attention.
4. Respect all safety rules to protect others.
5. Respect property. Cut living and dead trees only with permission and with good reason.
6. Subscribe to the Outdoor Code.

_____
Scout's signature

34234
2007 Boy Scouts of America

The Totin' Chip

For Woodwork requirement 1b you are to earn the Totin' Chip, which grants you the right to carry and use woods tools. See *The Boy Scout Handbook* for details.

Materials Needed

- [ ] One 1" x 8" board, at least 12" long
- [ ] One 1" x 2" board, at least 20" long
- [ ] One 3/8" dowel, 12" long
- [ ] Wood glue

Tools Needed

- [ ] Try square
- [ ] Pencil
- [ ] C-clamps
- [ ] Crosscut saw
- [ ] Tape measure or foot ruler
- [ ] Brace with 3/8" bit
- [ ] Mallet
- [ ] Block plane
- [ ] Small brush for spreading glue

Project 1: Make a Bench Hook

For your first woodworking project, try this bench hook. It's a tool you can build, then use again and again on future jobs. A bench hook helps you hold boards firmly in place on your workbench or other work surface to make sawing them easier.

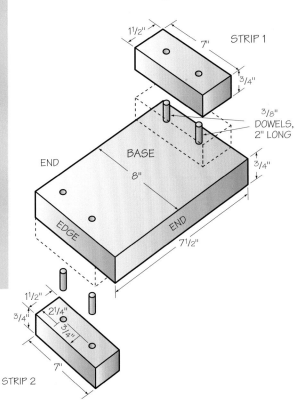

Steps for Making the Bench Hook

1. Check the 1" x 8" board for square. Square the board if necessary, as described in the previous section.

2. Measure 8" from the squared end and mark a point. Using the try square to guide your pencil, draw a line across the board's face, through the 8" mark.

3. Clamp the board to steady it. Saw along the pencil line. Set aside this 8" piece; it will be the base of your bench hook.

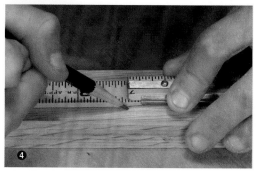

4. Square one end of the 1" x 2" board. From the squared board, measure, mark, and cut two strips 7" long.

5. On each strip, measure and mark the centers for two holes. The holes should be 2^1/$_4$" from each end and centered in the inch-and-a-half width of each strip, as shown in the drawing.

6. Lay a strip on the face of the 8" base piece. Align the strip's edge and one end flush with the base's edge and end, as shown.

7. Clamp the stacked pieces (7a) to your workbench (being sure to sandwich scrap wood between the base and the bench to protect your work surface). As you tighten the clamp,

keep the base and strip properly aligned, with their ends and edges flush. Then use your brace and $3/8$" bit to carefully drill each hole (7b). Drill completely through the strip *and* through the base, into the scrap wood beneath.

8. Unclamp the stacked pieces. Label and set aside the drilled strip (strip No. 1). Turn the base over.

9. Repeat steps 6 and 7, drilling through strip No. 2 and through the base at the opposite edge of the base.

10. From a $3/8$" dowel, cut four pieces, each 2" long.

11. Dry-fit the dowels. That is, try pushing them into the drilled holes to check for a snug fit, but do not push them so far in that you can't remove them. Pull them out before going to the next step.

12. Brush a little wood glue into the first two holes you drilled in the base (not too much glue—the excess will squeeze out). Spread a little glue on the bottom inch of a dowel. Insert the glued end of the dowel into a hole, and use a mallet to tap the dowel into place. Then glue and tap the bottom inch of a second dowel into the other prepared hole.

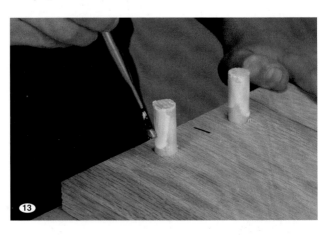

13. Using a brush, spread a thin layer of glue on the face of the base where strip No. 1 will sit. Brush glue onto the dowels that are sticking up from the base. Spread a layer of glue on the underside of the strip and inside the two holes in the strip.

14. With your hammer or mallet, tap the strip down over the two dowels (14a) until the underside of the strip is tight against the face of the base. The ends of the dowels should stick out of the holes a short way (14b). You made the dowels 2" long, and the combined thickness of the base and the strip is only $1^1/2$" ($^3/4$" plus $^3/4$").

15. Wipe away the excess glue while it is still wet.

16. Turn the base over.

17. Repeat steps 11 through 15 to fasten strip No. 2 to the other side of the base. The two strips must be on opposite faces of the base, as well as on opposite edges, as shown in the drawing.

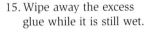

18. Clamp each strip to the base while the glue is drying. Allow the glue to dry completely before removing the clamps. (The photo shows only one strip in place.)

19. Finally, use a block plane to shave off the ends of the dowels that are sticking out of the holes.

Using Your Bench Hook

1. Put the bench hook on your work table so that strip No. 2 (the front strip) hooks over the table's front edge.

2. Lay a new board (lumber you intend to cut) on the bench hook's base.

3. Push the board's long edge up against strip No. 1 (the back strip). Be sure the end of the board hangs past the edge of the bench hook (and the edge of your work table) so you have room to saw.

4. Using the heel of your free hand, push the board tightly against the bench hook's back strip as you use your other hand to saw. Your bench hook will help you hold the board much steadier than you could hold it by hand alone.

A bench hook works best for cutting small stock and boards up to 3 feet long. Use a C-clamp to secure long boards before you saw them.

Glues and Adhesives

Woodworkers often use adhesives along with dowels, screws, nails, or other fasteners. Here are a few common types.

- **Polyvinyl (carpenter's wood)** glue is used mainly for furniture, craft, or general woodworking projects. It dries clear and won't stain, but it won't withstand water.

- **Resorcinol and formaldehyde** adhesive comes as two parts that must be mixed before using. Resorcinol glue is waterproof and heat resistant.

- **Contact** cements are used to bond veneers or to bond plastic laminates to wood for tabletops and counters. Align the surfaces perfectly before pressing them together because this adhesive will not pull apart.

- **Epoxy** resists almost anything, from water to solvents. Before using epoxy, as with all glues and adhesives, read the directions carefully. Follow instructions on how to mix the resin and the hardener and how long the mixture remains workable before it hardens.

Project 2: Make a "To-Do" List Holder

You need only a few inexpensive materials to make this holder for a to-do list (or a lumber-buying list). The plan calls for 1" x 6" lumber, but since you will be cutting the board down in width, you can use wider lumber (whatever you have in your scrap bin) and plane it down to the required dimensions.

Materials Needed

- [ ] One 1" x 6" (or wider) board, at least 27" long
- [ ] One $5/16$" dowel, $7^1/2$" long
- [ ] Wood glue
- [ ] Six finishing nails
- [ ] Metal cutting edge (serrated teeth) from a box of aluminum foil or plastic wrap, 5" long
- [ ] One roll of adding machine or printing calculator paper, 3" to $3^1/2$" wide (available from office supply stores)

Tools Needed

- [ ] Tape measure
- [ ] Pencil
- [ ] Straightedge (a 4-foot level, the long blade of a framing square, or the edge of a straight piece of lumber)
- [ ] C-clamps
- [ ] Vise
- [ ] Ripsaw
- [ ] Smoothing plane
- [ ] Try square
- [ ] Crosscut saw
- [ ] Brace with $3/8$" bit
- [ ] Coping saw
- [ ] Hand drill with $1/16$" bit
- [ ] Hammer

This list holder, when made as described, satisfies Woodwork requirement 4.

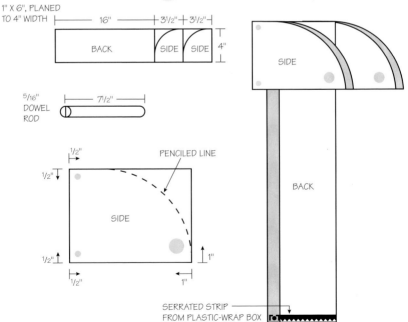

1" X 6", PLANED TO 4" WIDTH

16" ┤ 3¹/₂" ┤ 3¹/₂"

BACK | SIDE | SIDE | 4"

⁵/₁₆" DOWEL ROD

7¹/₂"

¹/₂"

¹/₂"

PENCILED LINE

SIDE

¹/₂"

¹/₂"

1"

1"

SIDE

BACK

SERRATED STRIP FROM PLASTIC-WRAP BOX

Steps for Making the List Holder

1. Measuring from the straight and square edge of the 1" x 6" board, mark a width of 4" near each end of the board.

2. Align a straightedge with the marks. Use it as a guide to pencil a line the length of the board.

3. Clamp the board to a secure work surface, making sure the pencil line clears the edge of the surface. With a ripsaw, saw off excess wood. Cut a little outside the pencil line, not exactly alongside it.

4. Turn the board so that the freshly cut edge is up. Secure it with clamps or in a vise. Plane the sawed edge lengthwise, removing wood down to the line.

> Sawing and planing to the pencil line will give you a 4"-wide board with straight edges.

5. Lay the board flat and check it for square. If necessary, square off one end.

6. Measure 3^1/$_2$" from the squared end. Using your try square and pencil, mark a cutting line.

7. Hold the board with your bench hook and saw along the pencil line. Save this 3^1/$_2$" piece; it will be one side of the list holder.

8. Repeat steps 6 and 7 to cut the second side piece.

9. Measure, mark, and cut the 16" back piece.

10. On each side piece, mark a point 1" in and 1" up from the outside bottom corner, as shown in the drawing (10a). Clamp for drilling, being sure to sandwich scrap wood between each side piece and the bench to protect your work surface. Drill the holes, using a brace and ^{3}/$_8$" bit. Drill completely through the side pieces, into the scrap wood beneath (10b).

11. Pencil a curved line on each side piece, starting above the hole and rounding to the upper edge, as shown in the drawing. Use a compass or the lip of a cup to guide your pencil.

12. Secure by clamping and cut along each curved line, using a coping saw.

13. With a hand drill and $^1/16$" bit, drill two pilot holes in each side piece, $^1/2$" from the edges as shown in the drawing.

14. To make a hanger hole in the back piece, use the brace and $^3/8$" bit to drill a hole about 1" from the top and centered side to side.

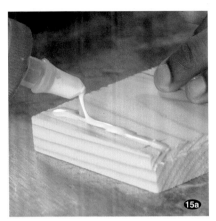

15. To assemble, clamp the back piece in a vise, one edge up. Apply a line of wood glue between and across the pilot holes in one side piece (15a). Glue the side piece into position, flush with the back piece. Secure the side to the back with a finishing nail through each pilot hole (15b).

16. Remove the assembly from the vise and flip it over, laying it on its side. Glue and nail the other side piece into position. Clamp the two sides to hold them tightly to the back until the glue is thoroughly dry.

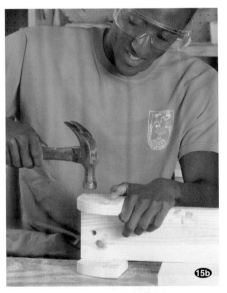

17. To finish the project, paint or stain the wood as desired. (See "Finishing Wood.") Then nail a metal cutting edge (taken from a box of aluminum foil or plastic wrap) near the bottom of the list holder. On the dowel rod, hang a roll of adding-machine paper between the side pieces, and slide the end of the paper between the wood and the cutting edge to hold it in place as you tear it off.

Project 3: Make a Wood Duck Nest Box

Materials

- [ ] One 1" x 12" board, 12' long
- [ ] 8d finishing nails
- [ ] 1/4" wire mesh hardware cloth
- [ ] Tacks
- [ ] One pair hinges with screws
- [ ] Two shutter hooks with roundhead screws

Tools Needed

- [ ] Square
- [ ] Tape measure
- [ ] Pencil
- [ ] C-clamps
- [ ] Crosscut saw
- [ ] Drill with 1/4" bit
- [ ] Compass
- [ ] Coping saw
- [ ] Hammer
- [ ] Screwdriver(s)

This big nest box is for wood ducks and hooded mergansers. Be sure to attach a 1/4" wire mesh inside the box below the entrance hole, as shown, so the ducklings can crawl out of the box after they hatch.

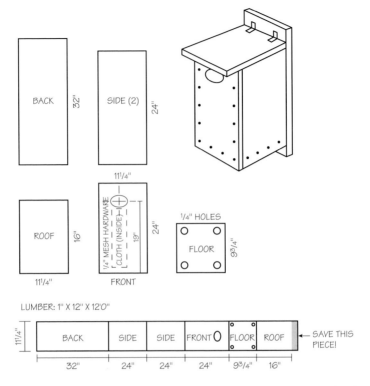

LUMBER: 1" X 12" X 12'0"

Drill pilot holes, as you did for project 2, to make your assembly easier. This nest box can also be assembled with wood screws through predrilled pilot holes.

Steps for Building the Nest Box

1. Measure (from the squared end of the board), mark, and cut the six pieces shown in the drawings.

2. Drill four $1/4$" drainage holes in the floor.

3. In the front piece, mark the location of the entrance hole (3a). Center the hole side-to-side and 19" up from the bottom. Use a compass (or a pattern made from paper) to draw an oval-shaped opening, 3" high and 4" wide (3b).

3a

3b

4. Drill a $1/4$" or slightly larger starter hole just inside the line.

5. Remove the blade from your coping saw, slip the blade through the starter hole, and reattach the blade to the saw frame. Cut out the entrance hole.

5

6. Tack a strip of hardware cloth under the hole.

7. Begin assembling the box by nailing the right side to the back panel. Nail through the back into the side piece.

8. Attach the floor to the right side and the back panel. Nail through the side and through the back into the floor.

9. Attach the left side, nailing through the back panel into the side piece and through the left side into the floor.

10. Attach the front (with the hardware cloth on the inside) by nailing through the front into the sides and floor.

11. Fasten the hinges to the roof.

12. Lay the roof in place on the box. Secure the hinges to the back panel.

13. Fasten shutter hooks to the roof and the sides, using roundhead screws, to hold the roof closed.

Insetting Hinges

Woodworkers and carpenters use many types of hinges, including T hinges, strap hinges, piano hinges, and butt hinges. In this pamphlet we deal only with butt hinges, one of the most popular types.

To install hinges, begin by setting the door or lid carefully into place. Position the hinges and mark the location on both the door or lid and on the frame or panel to which the hinges will attach. Mark the depth and width of the *gain*—the notch into which the hinge leaf fits.

Hold a chisel straight up and down with its blade just inside the cutting mark. Tap the chisel with a wooden mallet all along the mark to score (groove) the cutting line. Then chisel out the gain. The best way is to make a series of cuts with the chisel in the direction of the grain of the wood, by lightly tapping the chisel with a mallet. Then use a wide chisel to pare out the bottom of the gain.

When you have made the gains for each hinge, fasten the hinges with screws. It is a good idea to put only one screw in each hinge until you are sure no further fitting will be necessary. Then put in the remaining screws.

This nest box, if made with inset hinges, is a satisfactory project for Woodwork optional requirement 6c.

Project 4: Create Your Own

For requirement 5, you are to create your own carpentry project. Think of something fun to make or an item you want or need. A tool rack? Doghouse? Bird feeder?

Working Drawings

Whatever it is, start by sketching it out. Make the sort of *working drawings* you have used for the projects you have already built. As you have seen, working drawings are fairly detailed and accurate sketches of a project. They show the dimensions for each piece and how the pieces fit together.

Some working drawings show only two views, the front and the top or the front and one side. Others have three views—top, front, and side. Some detailed jobs for carpenters might require as many as six views. For your project, show as many views as you need to fully visualize the project, its dimensions, and how to cut and assemble the pieces.

Tool Rack

The sample bill of materials below lists everything needed (except fasteners—nails or screws) to build the tool rack illustrated.

Bill of Materials—Tool Rack

Quantity	Item/Use	Size	Length
7	Boards—framework for pegboard	1" x 2"	46$\frac{1}{2}$"
2	Boards—framework for pegboard	1" x 2"	72"
1	Board for the base	1" x 6"	72"
1	$\frac{1}{8}$" pegboard for the panel	4' x 6'	
20 linear feet	Molding		
6	Metal angles		

Bill of Materials

Also list the materials you will need. Your list (called a *bill of materials*) should show the sizes and lengths of all lumber required, as well as any hardware needed, such as hinges, hasps, locks, and knobs. Make up this bill of materials carefully. It will be your shopping list at the lumberyard or building center, and the best way of keeping track of the cost of the materials you use.

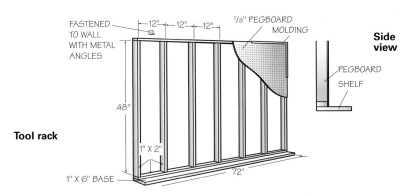

Recordkeeping

As you design and then build your project, keep track of the hours and money you spend, and keep your receipts. Record this information. Carpenters would not know how much to charge for their work if they had no record of their time or costs. Although you aren't doing this work for pay, it's still a good idea (and for requirement 5, it's a must) to get into the habit of keeping good records.

Project Ideas

Several possible carpentry projects are shown in this section. You can adapt them to your needs. Or check the *Home Repairs* merit badge pamphlet and other books listed in the resources section for more ideas.

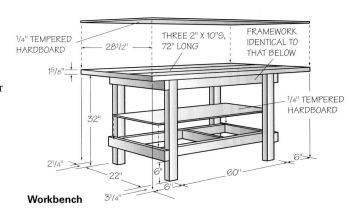

Sharpening block

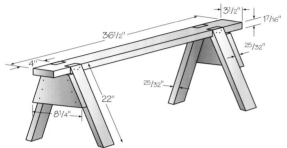

Use solid lumber for a sawhorse.

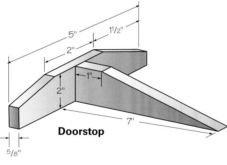

Doorstop

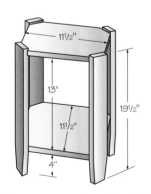

Use screws and good-quality lumber for a stool.

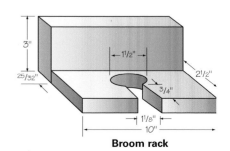

Broom rack

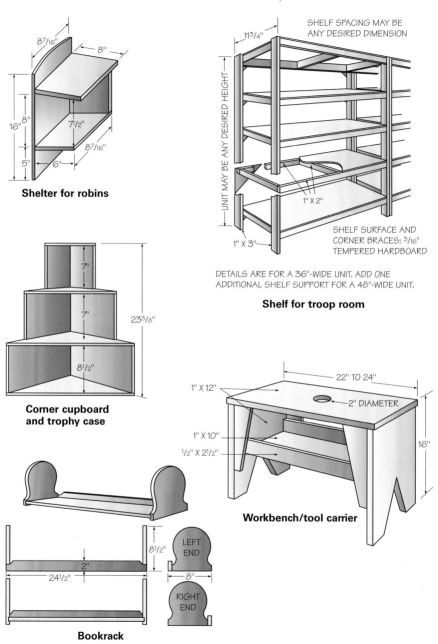

Shelter for robins

SHELF SPACING MAY BE ANY DESIRED DIMENSION

11³/₄"

UNIT MAY BE ANY DESIRED HEIGHT

1" X 2"

1" X 3"

SHELF SURFACE AND CORNER BRACES: ³/₁₆" TEMPERED HARDBOARD

DETAILS ARE FOR A 36"-WIDE UNIT. ADD ONE ADDITIONAL SHELF SUPPORT FOR A 48"-WIDE UNIT.

Shelf for troop room

Corner cupboard and trophy case

7"

7"

23³/₈"

8¹/₂"

Workbench/tool carrier

1" X 12"

2" DIAMETER

22" TO 24"

1" X 10"

¹/₂" X 2¹/₂"

16"

Bookrack

LEFT END

RIGHT END

8¹/₂"

2"

24¹/₂"

8"

Project 5: Fine Woodworking

The projects you have completed up to now probably have not called for much fine woodworking. Fulfilling requirement 6 gives you the chance to learn some of the more advanced skills that carpenters and cabinetmakers use.

Beveled and Rounded Edges

A *bevel* is an angle cut in a board, either to make it look better or to fit the board properly against another piece. A bevel is made by shaving the wood with a smoothing plane or block plane. Begin by drawing a line on the wood to show the angle to be cut. Then secure the piece in a vise and plane away the excess wood. Check your work frequently to make sure you are not planing too much.

Rounding an edge is simply another step beyond beveling. Instead of leaving a sharp edge, plane it down to a rounded shape. Then sand the edge to smooth and further round it, being sure to sand with the wood's grain.

Bevel

Curved and Incised Cuttings

Some projects may call for cutting wood in curved or irregular shapes or making *incised* (deeply and sharply notched) cuttings in the edges of the wood. As you have learned already, a coping saw is good for making curved cuts. So is a power jigsaw.

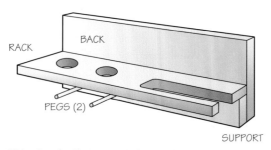

This sketch shows a rack for holding a baseball bat, balls, and mitts.

Joints

The most familiar way to join two pieces of wood is the *butt joint,* in which the pieces are simply butted together at right angles and held by nails, screws, or some other type of fastener. You have made several butt joints in your projects so far.

If you built the bench hook, you have also made a *face joint.* A face joint is two boards fastened together so that their faces are flat against each other. Here are some other types of joints that woodworkers use.

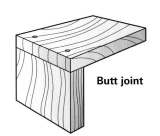

Butt joint

Face joint

Miter Joint

The angled *miter joint* is especially useful where two pieces come together at a corner and you do not want the end grain of either piece to show. Miter joints are used on picture frames, trims, door moldings, and similar projects where appearance counts.

For a joint in which the two pieces make a square corner (an angle of 90 degrees, also called a right angle), each piece must be cut to a 45-degree angle. To make precise cuts use a *miter box,* which has slits for guiding the saw at exactly the correct angle.

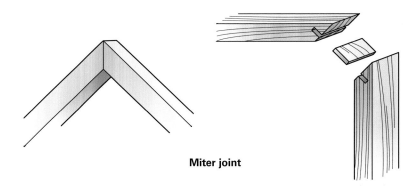

Miter joint

A miter joint, even when nailed, is not very strong. To reinforce it, woodworkers often use a corner brace made of metal, or a wooden *spline.* A spline is a thin, flat piece of wood that is glued into grooves in the two pieces being joined. The spline adds strength to the joint.

Dowel Joint

Dowels can be used as fasteners for different types of joints. You could use a dowel in place of a spline, for instance, in a large miter joint. In building the bench hook, you used dowels to fasten the face joints.

Dowels are used in fine furniture making to join the edges of two pieces of wood for a strong, neat joint. The steps are:

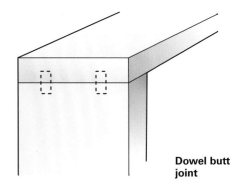

Dowel butt joint

1. Drill holes, using an auger bit of the same size as the dowels, in the edges of the two pieces.

2. Spread glue over the dowels and the edges.

3. Drive the dowels into the holes in one piece of wood.

4. Press the other piece of wood onto the dowels where their ends are sticking out of the holes.

5. Clamp the whole assembly until the glue dries.

A new approach to the traditional technique of the dowel joint is called *biscuit* (or *plate*) *joinery.* "Biscuits" are essentially flat dowels: thin, football-shaped pieces of compressed beechwood that are glued into slots much as dowels are glued into holes. A special machine called a biscuit (or plate) joiner cuts a crescent-shaped slot in each of the pieces that are to be joined. The slots can also be made using a router with a biscuit-cutter bit. You may substitute biscuits for dowels to satisfy requirement 6a if you have access to the necessary equipment.

Mortise and Tenon Joint

A mortise and tenon joint has two parts: the *mortise* is a hole in one piece of wood, and the *tenon* is the part of the second piece that is cut and shaped to fit into the mortise. Simply, this joint is "a square peg in a square hole."

To start the mortise, drill the holes only as deep as you want the mortise to be. Then use a sharp wood chisel to shave out any excess wood and square the corners. To make the tenon, mark its depth and width on the end of the tenon piece. Use a backsaw to cut the tenon, making a series of straight, square cuts to remove excess wood.

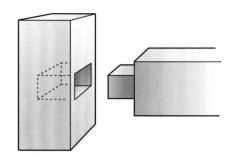

Think of "tenant"—someone who dwells inside a place—to help you remember that the *tenon* (the peg) goes inside the *mortise* (the hole).

Project Ideas

For requirement 6a, you might choose a project below, take an idea from a book or Web site listed in the resources section, or think of something on your own. Whatever your project, make working drawings before you begin building it.

- A picture frame with miter joints and/or beveled edges

- A stool with rounded edges and/or mortise and tenon joints

- Wall shelves with mortise and tenon or dowel joints

- A small table with a round top and dowel fastenings for legs and top

- A three-legged coffee table with a curved top, as illustrated

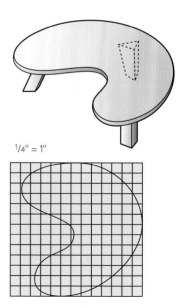

$1/4" = 1"$

Project 6: Turning Wood on a Lathe

A *wood-turning lathe* shapes wood into rounded forms by spinning it against a cutting edge handheld by a woodworker. To turn wood on a lathe for optional requirement 6b, you must have access to a lathe, either at home or in school. An adult who is completely familiar with the lathe's operation should help you with this project.

Here are some beginner projects you may want to try.

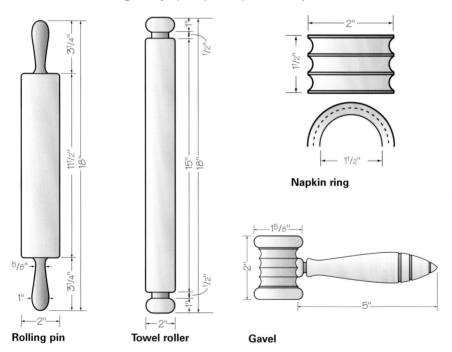

Rolling pin   **Towel roller**   **Napkin ring**   **Gavel**

Dimensions for a rolling pin, towel roller, napkin ring, and gavel

Wood-Turning Tools

Gouges are used in several sizes, from 1/8 inch to 2 inches. The larger ones are for rough cuts; the small ones are for tiny grooves.

The cutting edge of a **skew chisel** is at an angle with one of the sides. It is used to make a sharp cut after the gouges have done the rough cutting work.

A **roundnose chisel** is used mostly for making rounded grooves. It may also be used for rough work.

The **parting tool** makes cuts with square sides and bottoms.

Gouges

Skew chisel

The **caliper** is a measuring tool used to check the diameter of the work on the lathe.

Parting tool (top view) **Parting tool (side view)**

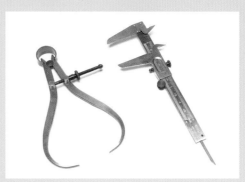

Calipers

The **headstock** on a lathe holds the revolving spindle. **Lathe centers,** which fit in the headstock and tailstock spindles, hold the wood stock so it can be turned and worked. The headstock spindle center is called the **live center** because it revolves with the work. The **tailstock,** the adjustable part of a lathe, supports the **dead center,** so named because it does not turn. Instead, the wood revolves on the dead center.

Preparing the Job

The wood block to be turned (the wood stock) should be square or nearly square and about an inch longer than the finished piece is to be. Begin by drawing diagonal lines from corner to corner on each end of the stock (1). This locates the center of the stock.

Take the *live center* off the lathe (2). With a wooden mallet, drive its spur firmly into the center of one end of the stock (3). (If the wood is hard, make shallow saw cuts along the diagonals and drill a small hole in the center before you try to drive home the live center.) Now take the live center out of the wood and put it back in the *headstock* of the lathe.

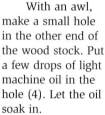

With an awl, make a small hole in the other end of the wood stock. Put a few drops of light machine oil in the hole (4). Let the oil soak in.

Now bring the wood to the lathe and fit the grooved end against the live center (5). Hold that end in place and move the *tailstock* assembly to about an inch from the other end of the wood. Clamp it

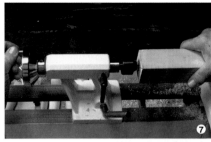

in place (6). Turn the handwheel on the tailstock to move it toward the wood and guide the hole onto the *dead center* until the piece is firmly held by the lathe (7). Lock the handwheel (8).

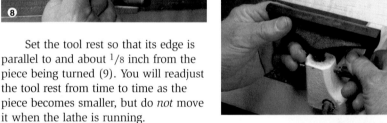

Set the tool rest so that its edge is parallel to and about $^1/_8$ inch from the piece being turned (9). You will readjust the tool rest from time to time as the piece becomes smaller, but do *not* move it when the lathe is running.

Holding the Tools

Hold all tools firmly but not rigidly. Grasp the handle of the tool at the extreme end (1). This gives the most leverage and lessens the possibility of the tool being thrown from your hand. Also, if you hold the tool  this way, any slight wavering of your hand will not cause as much variance in the work as it would if you held the tool shorter.

Use your other hand as a guide, holding it palm down over the tool near the cutting edge, with the little finger and the back part of the palm touching the tool rest (2).

Making the Roughing Cut

After you place the wood stock in the lathe, turn on the power. Then place the large gouge on the tool rest with the bevel above the

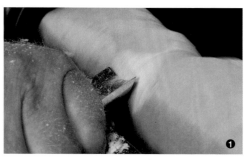

wood and the cutting edge touching the piece being turned. Keep the handle down. Roll the gouge over lightly to the right to make a shearing cut rather than a scraping one (1). Lift the handle slowly and force the cutting edge deep enough into the piece to remove all the corners (2).

Begin this operation about $3/4$ inch from the dead center end, and do the same thing about every $3/4$ inch for the entire length of the stock (3). This way, you will avoid the danger of breaking off large slivers.

Now work the tool back and forth from one end to the other until the diameter of the stock is slightly larger than required (4). As you move the tool back and forth,

hold it at a slight angle to the axis of the cylinder of wood, and keep the cutting point always slightly in advance of the handle (5).

Tip: Stock that is too dry does not turn as well as stock with some moisture in it.

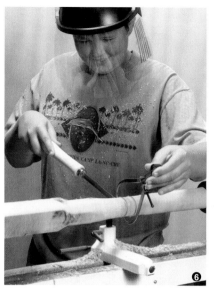

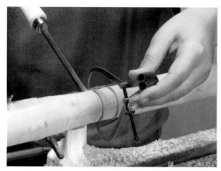

Now set the caliper to the required diameter. Holding the small gouge in the right hand, make grooves about 1 inch apart the entire length of the stock, at the same time holding the caliper in the left hand perpendicular to the cylinder (6). Cut each groove until the caliper slips over the stock. This is the *sizing cut.*

Making the Smoothing Cut

Place the skew chisel on the tool rest with the cutting edge above the cylinder of wood and forming an angle of about 60 degrees with the surface (1). Slowly raise the handle and at the same time draw the chisel back until it begins to cut.

Start about 3 inches from either end and move toward the near end. Then start at the same point and cut toward the other end (2). Continue this process until the entire surface is smooth and all traces of the sizing cuts are removed.

Use a straightedge to test the cylinder for accuracy. Test for smoothness with the palm of the hand, first stopping the lathe. *NEVER test for smooth-ness while the work is rotating.*

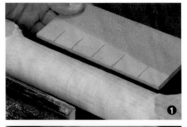

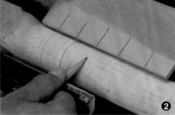

Cutting Shoulders

Turn (cut) the stock down to the largest diameter required in the piece you are making.

Then mark off, on a stick of about the same length as the cylinder, all lines indicating shoulders, or "bulges" (1). Holding the stick against the cylinder, transfer these lines to the wood by touching a pencil against it at the proper points (2).

Turn all shoulders down to the required diameter (3), measuring them with your caliper.

When you are making duplicate turnings, it helps to have several sets of calipers. At the start, set them for the various diameters called for in the finished piece.

To cut *convex* (rounded up) surfaces between shoulders, first cut down to the center of the convex surface or *head*. Mark this center with a pencil (4). Using a small skew chisel, cut from this center, first to one side, then to the other. Use the heel of the tool for this operation (5).

Cut *concave* (rounded in) surfaces with a medium-sized gouge, cutting from the outside to the center (6). *Never try to follow through the center and come up on the other side.* There is a danger of the tool catching when cutting against the grain.

Squaring Off Ends

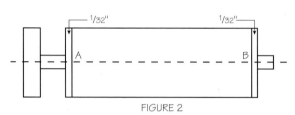

FIGURE 1

LIVE CENTER   DEAD CENTER

FIGURE 2

1. Turn (cut) the cylinder of wood to the correct diameter. Then lay out pencil lines on the job as shown in figure 1.

2. With the parting tool, cut the ends down to $1/2$" diameter, $1/32$" outside lines A and B, as shown in figure 2.

3. With the toe of the skew chisel, make cuts to lines A and B. Swing the handle of the skew chisel out. The ends should be flat.

4. You still have $1/2$-inch-diameter waste stock at each end to take off. Start at the dead center end and make V cuts to reduce the wood to $1/8$ inch in diameter. Do the same at the live center end. Cut off this last $1/8$ inch with a knife.

Rules for Lathe Work

- Oil the lathe every day before starting. After finishing, brush the lathe clean of all shavings and wipe off surplus oil. Clean the tools and put them in their proper places.

- Keep tools sharp. Dull tools will not make smooth cuts.

- Before turning the lathe on, slowly turn rough materials a few times to be sure they will clear the tool rest.

- Wear a full-face shield whenever you are operating a lathe.

- Do not wear loose clothing. Button your sleeves or roll them above the elbow. Tie back long hair.

- Start all jobs at the lowest speed. For rough work, run the lathe at slow speed. Increase the speed as the work gets smoother.

- Never touch the stock when it is moving.

Project 7: Wooden Toys or Service Project

For optional requirement 6d, your merit badge counselor or Scoutmaster may suggest a Good Turn that you and your buddies can do. Your school or religious institution or the organization that operates your troop may have some carpentry work that needs doing.

If you would like to make wooden toys, discuss your ideas with your Scoutmaster or counselor. Either of them can help you deliver your creations to children who will love them. You may want to donate the toys through an organization that serves underprivileged families.

Paddle Boat

Your local library probably will have books with plans for making wooden toys. A few such books are listed in the resources section of this pamphlet. The paddle boat shown here is a good project to start with; it has a rubber-band "motor."

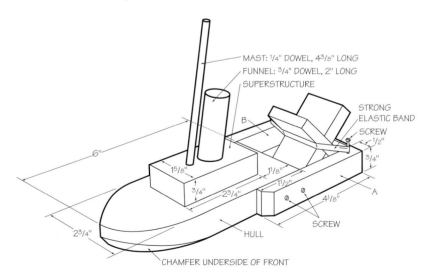

Steps for Making the Paddle Boat

1. Cut and shape the hull as shown.

2. Shape paddle stays A and B. Using brass screws (which do not rust), screw the paddle stays onto the sides of the hull.

3. Drill shallow holes at a slight angle in the superstructure to hold the funnel and mast. Glue the funnel and mast dowels in place.

4. Glue the superstructure to the hull.

5. Make the paddle from two pieces of $^3/8$" plywood. Using a backsaw, cut a $^3/8$" x $^3/4$" slot in each, as shown. Remove waste wood with a small chisel. Fit and glue the pieces together. Allow the glue to dry thoroughly.

6. Varnish or paint the boat and the paddle to protect the wood from water.

7. Insert two brass screws in the upper ends of the paddle stays, as shown, to hold an elastic band. Fit the paddle in place between the stays, held by the elastic band.

8. Wind up the paddle until the elastic band is fully stretched. Put the boat in water and release. (A strong, thick band will move the boat quickly over a short distance. A thinner band produces less speed but longer range. Experiment to find the best size.)

Cutting List

1 hull, 6" x $2^3/4$" x $^3/4$"

1 superstructure,
   $2^3/4$" x $1^5/8$" x $^3/4$"

1 funnel, 2" x $^3/4$"-
   diameter dowel

1 mast, $4^3/8$" x $^1/4$"-
   diameter dowel

2 paddle stays,
   $4^1/8$" x $^3/4$" x $^1/2$"

2 paddles,
   $2^3/4$" x $1^3/8$" x $^3/8$"
   plywood

Other materials:

brass screws, wood glue, varnish or paint, elastic bands (various sizes)

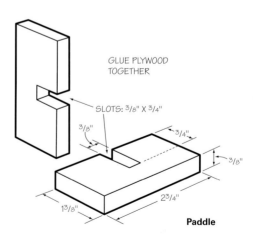

GLUE PLYWOOD
TOGETHER

SLOTS: $^3/8$" X $^3/4$"

$^3/8$"

$^3/4$"

$^3/8$"

$2^3/4$"

$1^3/8$"

Paddle

Finishing Wood

The final step in a woodworking project is *finishing,* that is, removing or covering blemishes, smoothing the surface, and protecting or coloring the wood with a treatment such as paint or stain.

Removing or Covering

Use a wood filler to fill and cover imperfections in the wood such as knots and small knotholes. Set nails (drive them below the wood's surface with a nailset) and fill the holes with wood filler. Also fill countersunk screw heads.

Sanding

Sanding removes tool marks and smoothes wood surfaces. Always sand *with* the grain of the wood. For flat surfaces use a sanding block. If you don't have a store-bought sanding block, make one from a block of wood about 6" x 3 1/2" x 1". Pad the top and bottom with cork or felt to protect the work. Wrap the sandpaper around the block and hold it against the sides of the block as you work.

Sandpapers come in different *grits,* or textures, from coarse to super fine. The higher the grit number, the finer the sandpaper. Which grit you use depends on the wood and on the work you are doing. In general, start sanding with a coarser sandpaper and then finish with a finer paper.

For most projects, you will finish sanding with a 150- or 180-grit sandpaper. The higher grits are mostly used for putting an exceptionally smooth surface on fine woodwork and furniture.

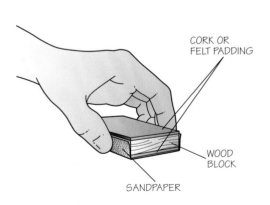

CORK OR
FELT PADDING

WOOD
BLOCK

SANDPAPER

Use the following table as a guide for choosing the right sandpaper for the job.

Grit	Common Name	Uses
40–60	Coarse	Heavy sanding and stripping; roughing the surface
80–120	Medium	Removing tool marks and minor imperfections; smoothing the surface
150–180	Fine	Final sanding before applying a finish
220–240	Very fine	Sanding between coats of stain or sealer
280–320	Extra fine	Removing dust spots or marks between finish coats
360–600	Super fine	Fine sanding of the finish to dull the luster or remove shallow scratches

Sandpapers come in different types as well as different grits. The two types that woodworkers use most are *aluminum oxide* and *garnet.* Aluminum oxide is long-lasting and usually used with power sanders. Most papers meant for hand sanding have particles of garnet, a natural abrasive.

Protecting and Coloring

The finish you put on a project depends on the project and on your personal tastes and preferences. **Wood stain** brings out the beauty of the grain and enhances the wood's natural color. **Paint** (enamel, for example) covers and hides the wood and can color it almost any shade imaginable. **Varnish, shellac,** and **lacquer** give a hard, glossy finish while exposing the beauty of the wood. **Wax** protects varnish and will polish to a smooth, shiny finish.

Use a good quality brush for staining, painting, and varnishing, and be sure to clean your brush in the proper solvent as soon as you are done.

If you are undecided about a finish, talk with your merit badge counselor, the shop teacher at school, or a salesperson at a paint store. They may suggest suitable finishes and how to apply them. Your project might require a filler coat or sealer before you apply the finish. For a beautifully varnished surface, you might apply three or four coats, sanding (after the varnish dries) with extra-fine sandpaper between coats. Ask the advice of someone knowledgeable. Also see "Painting, Staining, and Varnishing Wood" in the "Home Furnishings How-Tos" section of the *Home Repairs* merit badge pamphlet.

Careers for Woodworkers

If you like working with wood, you might consider doing it for a living. Many opportunities exist. Some woodworkers work in sawmills and plywood mills. Some make furniture and kitchen cabinets. Some make baseball bats, racquets, oars, toys, tool handles, and musical instruments. Some operate machines that cut, assemble, and finish raw wood to make doors, windows, flooring, paneling, molding, and trim for new homes.

Carpenters, of course, also work with wood. *Rough carpenters* assemble the frameworks of buildings and cover the frames with sheathing, siding, and shingles. *Finish carpenters* do the interior work of hanging doors and windows, installing paneling and trim, laying floors, building stairs, and hanging kitchen cabinets. Some carpenters help to build bridges, docks, industrial plants, and ships.

Training

Woodworkers and carpenters learn their trades through both on-the-job training and classroom study. Some attend a technical or vocational school. Becoming a skilled woodworker often takes at least two years after high school. To prepare, you should take math, science, and computer classes in school, and also shop and mechanical drawing.

The United Brotherhood of Carpenters and Joiners of America; Associated General Contractors Inc. (AGC); and the National Association of Home Builders offer apprenticeship programs. In addition, local chapters of the Associated Builders and Contractors, as well as the AGC have training programs that combine on-the-job training with classroom work. Check the resources section for the addresses and Web sites of these organizations.

To learn carpentry, an apprentice-ship may be best. Apprentices learn on duty, and they also have classes in safety, first aid, blueprint reading, freehand sketching, basic math, and different carpentry techniques. Usually, apprentices must be at least 17 years old and meet local require-ments. For example, some union locals test an applicant's aptitude for carpentry. Apprenticeship programs usually last three or four years.

The Work

Many occupations for woodworkers and carpenters are physically demanding. You will need to be fit, with a good sense of balance and good eye-hand coordination. You also will need an eye for detail, patience, and the ability to work from a blue-print or scale drawing and to follow detailed instructions and specifications.

When the economy slows and little construction work is available, steady work for carpenters can be unpredictable. Carpenters who know how to do any kind of carpentry have the best chances for staying busy. They may build, repair, or remodel homes, schools, or offices, doing various jobs from rough framing to fine finishing work. Carpenters with all-around skills can usually find a new assignment when they have finished their current one, or they can set up shop for themselves.

Highly skilled custom woodworkers and cabinetmakers often open their own shops. They specialize in making one-of-a-kind furniture and other items, often using traditional hand tools and portable power tools. Production woodworkers, on the other hand, may operate high-speed computer-controlled machines to turn out lots of identical wooden parts. Many processes in mills and manufacturing plants are now automated. This means that woodworkers with computer skills are increasingly in demand.

To Learn More

Working conditions and wages vary considerably in different parts of the United States. A local carpenter or cabinetmaker will be able to tell you about your area. To ask about apprentice-ships or other career opportunities, contact local building con-tractors or the United Brotherhood of Carpenters and Joiners of America. (See the resources section.) For more information about woodworking occupations, check with cabinetmakers, *millwork* firms, furniture makers, sawmills, or lumber dealers in your area.

Millwork: doors, sashes, base-boards, trim, mantels, or other products made by machine.

Resources for Woodworking

Scouting Literature

Deck of First Aid; Emergency First Aid pocket guide; *Be Prepared First Aid Book; Drafting, First Aid, Forestry, Home Repairs, Model Design and Building, Painting, Pulp and Paper,* and *Wood Carving* merit badge pamphlets

Visit the Boy Scouts of America's official retail Web site at *http://www.scoutstuff.org* for a complete listing of all merit badge pamphlets and other helpful Scouting materials and supplies.

Books

Adkins, Jan. *Toolchest.* Walker, 1984.

Bramlett, Tim. *A Kid's Guide to Crafts: Wood Projects.* Stackpole Books, 1997.

Creative Publishing. *The Complete Guide to Easy Woodworking Projects.* Creative Publishing, 2003.

Fine Woodworking. *The Basics of Craftsmanship: Key Advice on Every Aspect of Woodworking.* Taunton, 2003.

Fraser, Aime. *Getting Started in Woodworking: Skill-Building Projects That Teach the Basics.* Taunton, 2003.

McGuire, Kevin. *Woodworking for Kids: 40 Fabulous, Fun & Useful Things for Kids to Make.* Sterling, 1994.

Nelson, John R. *American Folk Toys: Easy-to-Build Toys for Kids of All Ages.* Taunton, 1998.

Magazines

American Woodworker
Telephone: 952-948-5890
Web site:
http://www.americanwoodworker.com

Popular Woodworking
F + W Publications, Inc.
Web site:
http://www.popularwoodworking.com

Videos

Basic Carpentry. D.I.Y. Video, 1985.

Easy Woodworking Projects. D.I.Y. Video, 1985.

Small Shop Projects: Boxes. Taunton Press, 1990.

Woodworking Made Easy With Hank Metz, Vol. 1: Biscuit Joinery Techniques. Easyway Ventures, 1996.

Organizations and Web Sites

Absolutely Free Plans
Web site:
http://absolutelyfreeplans.com

Bureau of Labor Statistics
U.S. Department of Labor
Web site:
http://www.bls.gov/oco/ocos202.htm

National Association of Home Builders
1201 15th St. NW
Washington, DC 20005
Toll-free telephone: 800-368-5242
Web site: *http://www.nahb.org*

Sawdust Making 101
Web site:
http://www.sawdustmaking.com

United Brotherhood of Carpenters and Joiners of America
101 Constitution Ave. NW
Washington, DC 20001
Telephone: 202-546-6206
Web site: *http://www.carpenters.org*

WoodNet.net
Web site: *http://www.woodnet.net/tips*

WoodZone.com
Web site: *http://www.woodzone.com*

Acknowledgments

The Boy Scouts of America thanks skilled woodworkers Michael Rosenberg and Robert Meunier of the Charlotte (North Carolina) Woodworkers Association who so graciously assisted us with this new edition of the *Woodwork* merit badge pamphlet. We appreciate their knowledge and expertise on the subject very much, and we are grateful for the time they took to help us.

The BSA is thankful for the work of the American Library Association, which helped update the resources section of this pamphlet. The ALA has a committee that is charged with assisting the merit badge pamphlet series in this capacity, and it does so very effectively.

Photo and Illustration Credits

HAAP Media Ltd., courtesy—cover *(chisel/shavings)*

©Photos.com—cover *(level, bench, tape measure, hammer/nail)*; pages 4, 6 *(background)*, 19 *(top)*, 20 *(bottom left, bottom right)*, 23 *(both at bottom)*, and 76–77 *(both)*

All other photos and illustrations not mentioned above are the property of or are protected by the Boy Scouts of America.

Daniel Giles—cover *(nest box)*; pages 10, 18, 45 *(top)*, 46–50 *(all)*, 51 *(bottom)*, and 52–55 *(all)*

John McDearmon—all illustrations

Notes